FACE TO FACE WITH
LIONS

by Beverly and Dereck Joubert

NATIONAL
GEOGRAPHIC
WASHINGTON, D.C.

Beverly and me in the bush, tracking lions.

FACE TO FACE

Showing a perfect set of teeth, this lion's yawn sends a clear message: Any attacker will face powerful weapons of defense.

Most people don't really like getting up close and personal with lions. And that's a good thing, because lions are dangerous.

In many places in Africa, lions have attacked and killed people. But lions are not out to get you! They just want to mind their own business and stay out of trouble.

My wife Beverly and I have spent more than 25 years studying, filming, and photographing lions—and trying to steer clear of their teeth. But

HOW NOT TO GET EATEN BY A LION

■ Lions are quite polite, and they expect the same from you. Never approach one directly from the front. You may be telling him you want to fight! Don't sneak up on him either.

■ Wide eyes are a threat to a lion. Squint when you look at one. Never look at it directly.

■ Don't run when you are around lions. They're cats, and cats love to chase. Back away slowly.

we've never had any major problems with lions. Maybe it's because we know them so well. We've spent so much of our lives with them.

Sometimes, coming face to face with lions can be a little too exciting. One day, we accidentally came upon a pair of lions mating. Usually this is no problem if you give way, but the male was new in the area. We didn't know him, and he didn't know us. He charged from 600 feet (almost 200 meters), the longest charge I have ever seen.

We live by an important rule out here. If a lion charges, we stand our ground. If we ran, it would turn into a cat-and-mouse game. And that's a game we couldn't win. So we faced down the angry lion. At 300 feet (90 meters), he was showing no signs of giving up.

I said quietly to Beverly at my side, "Steady, just wait." She didn't break the silence. At 150 feet (45 meters), after what seemed like an eternity, I could see his bared yellow teeth and the amber red fire in his eyes. When he growled, I could smell his breath. "Steady," I said. Beverly was dead quiet. We were at the top of a 10-foot-high (3-meter) riverbank, and I thought that he would stop at the bottom. Instead, he powered up, kicking and snarling and clawing at the sand.

Finally, to my surprise, I saw one of his hefty paws come up over the ridge. He was not more than a lion's leap away as he tried to haul himself over the edge—right at me.

Almost in slow motion, the sandy bank at my feet pulled away. The lion fell back. As he looked up at me, his eyes showed a flicker of disappointment. Then he turned away.

He slowly walked back to his female, who was growling in approval. No doubt, she was quite impressed.

It was only then that I discovered why Beverly had been so quiet. She wasn't there! Only her two shoes next to me marked the spot where she had stood.

Then I realized that she had probably done the right thing by slowly backing away. My brave showdown with the lion now seemed pretty dumb. It is silly to test your strength against a lion.🐾

MEET

THE LION

◄ Frisky lion cubs are always attacking their mothers, leaping on their heads or ambushing their tails. Play is a way for young ones to learn the moves of a hunt, chase, and kill. But at first they may only hunt their poor mother's tattered ear!

◄ Mischief comes in small bundles. A male cub squeezes past his sister's legs to steal their mother's attention. Lions bond through touching, rubbing against each other, and grooming.

In all our years in Africa, we've been attacked by elephants, and a grumpy buffalo once bumped the car we were riding in. We've had close calls with snakes and scorpions. We've also had malaria and other diseases. But we've never had any major problems with the lions whom we have spent so much of our lives living with. Maybe it's because we know lions so well.

Lions live mainly in Africa. They range from the Skeleton Coast in Namibia, through the great

9

Okavango Delta in Botswana, up into East Africa, and even into the forests of West Africa. A small number live in India. In each place they're different. For example, in the great plains of East Africa, you can see lions lolling around in the sun and hunting in the daylight. But in Botswana's Savute region, they usually hunt at night.

⬆ *Lions once ranged across the entire African continent, but they have been eliminated in the north and far south.*

➡ *The vast plains of the Okavango Delta make a magical backdrop for lions. More than 3,000 lions live here, not far from our camp.*

Lions are known scientifically as *Panthera leo*. To understand them, you have to realize that they are predatory carnivores. That means they eat meat, and they have to kill to survive. But they are also picky eaters. In one area, they may hunt elephants for six weeks each year. In the Duba Plains, where we live now, they hunt only buffalo and

Lions mate in a courtship of flashing teeth and growling that can last up to a week. Cubs are born about three and a half months later.

Mothers hide their cubs, moving them often so hyenas don't find them and kill them. When the cubs are a month or two old, their mom brings them into the pride.

would never eat anything as tough as elephant. They are adaptable, eating antelope in one area and living off seals on the beaches in another.

Lion families are called prides. A pride of lions is usually made up of six to eight females, two males, and up to 24 cubs (or none at all). Each female can have four to six cubs at a time.

We love to watch lions with cubs. Sometimes you'll see the cubs running, leaping, biting an ear, attacking a tail. The cubs in a pride are usually born around the same time. They suckle the milk from any mother they come across at any time. After three or four months, I doubt whether the mothers even know which cubs are theirs.🐾

↑ By the age of a year, male and female cubs will join in all the activities of the pride. They even go along on hunts. In Duba, where we live, that means wading through water—although from the looks on their faces and their flattened-back ears, it seems like these "teenagers" are not that happy about getting their feet wet.

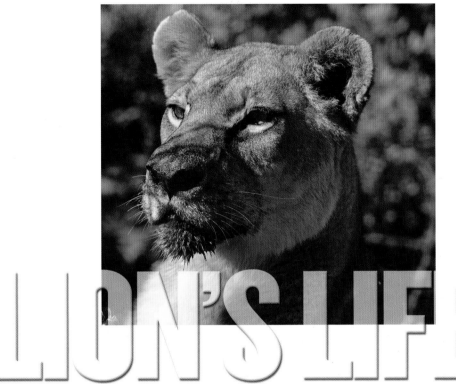

← Lions, like all predators, have evolved to eat meat. It's the only way they can get enough energy to live. They tend to be messy eaters.

A LION'S LIFE

← The kill. We are finding out that large predators are necessary for a healthy environment. Without them, herds of prey animals like zebras grow too large for the land to support. They eat all the plants, and the grassy plains can become a desert.

Being a lion must be wonderful, even though it is quite a short life. Lions can live about 15 years in the wild, but the oldest lion we ever filmed was 14 years old. One day while we were filming him, he walked toward us, fell over, and died.

Male lions leave their mother when they are about age three, and the brothers wander around together as nomads for two years. This means they move from place to place, not settling in one area.

Eventually, the brothers arrive in some far-off

Lionesses hunt together, with each one doing the job she's best at. Older individuals stalk and separate one prey animal from the herd. Younger, faster ones give chase and leap on the prey.

territory ready to challenge and fight for a new domain. Fights are usually brief—and dangerous. Lions are the heaviest cats in Africa. They are armed with long, strong teeth and razor-sharp claws, so even the winner can get badly injured. In fact, a lion would rather not fight. He prefers to roar and scare off his opponent if he can. So there is usually a lot of growling and spitting and hissing, and quite a bit of slapping.

That shaggy mane of hair can form a scarf of protection around the throat. But females fight as well, so a mane can't have evolved solely as a defense. Scientists believe that a mane has many functions. A lion's long dark mane sends a clear signal to any intruders that this is his territory and that these females are claimed by a strong, healthy male. Females also seem to prefer males with darker, longer manes. These shaggy-haired males also

⬆ *Against massive opponents like a bull buffalo, lions have to cooperate. All the lionesses of this pride must be fit and healthy and working together to bring down prey of this size. It's a real struggle!*

It's not easy being a super predator. Hyenas sense that this lioness is injured. They gather to test her strength. At any sign of weakness, these clever and competitive predators will attack even the strongest cat in Africa.

seem to keep their prides together the longest. But there's a cost to being the handsomest male— these big manes can also cause heat stress.

Even with his wild mane, the leader of a pride usually holds that rank for only two or three years. Then an outside challenger comes along and takes over.

Male lions that are beaten and thrown out of a pride often lose their manes. It's nature's way of helping them blend in and avoid attention from other lions.

For a lion, no day is really complete without hunting. We have been filming some amazing buffalo hunts lately. The lions of Duba are huge, and they hunt in and out of water. Most cats hate the water, but these lions have adapted completely to the swampy conditions. One time, we saw lions attack a huge buffalo. They fought him for seven hours, thrashing in and out of the water, before the kill.

In Botswana, after the lions have worked hard for their meal and are just about to enjoy it, the hyenas arrive. Now, lions weigh almost twice as much as hyenas. But when hyenas get the scent of blood and have all their clan members by their side, they will swoop down and attack anyway. Hyena clans can have as few as 10 or as many as 90 individuals. They can intimidate or bully the lions into sharing their kill. The hyenas can even send the lions running for the trees. But sometimes it's the other way around. Every once in a while, lions get to feast for free on kills that were brought down by hyenas.

HOW TO LIVE WITH LIONS

When you're staying on the African plains, or "in the bush," you are far away from the comforts of home.

▬ You live in a tent. A futon mattress makes a good bed.

▬ All your water comes from the river—for bathing, washing clothes, and drinking. Be careful near the water though—sometimes crocodiles will attack!

▬ We've even used our jeep as a stove. We wrap food in aluminum foil and cook it on the hot engine. If the gravy spills, it smells good!

Every boss has a successful huntress behind him. Although male lions rule, females make 90 percent of all lion kills.

THE FUTURE

Lord and master of the savanna! Male lions dominate their prides. They sleep most of the day. They get to eat first at kills. They mate with all the females of the pride, and every cub obeys them.

Lions have their own language, and if you read the signals, you can understand it, too. Humans don't always grasp the way things work in the lion kingdom, or they choose not to.

For example, when safari hunters shoot lions for recreation or sport, they usually select males with the biggest manes. But when they kill these big lions, they leave the pride with its smaller males. These lions with the smaller manes send a mixed signal across the savanna. It says, "I'm here, but I

21

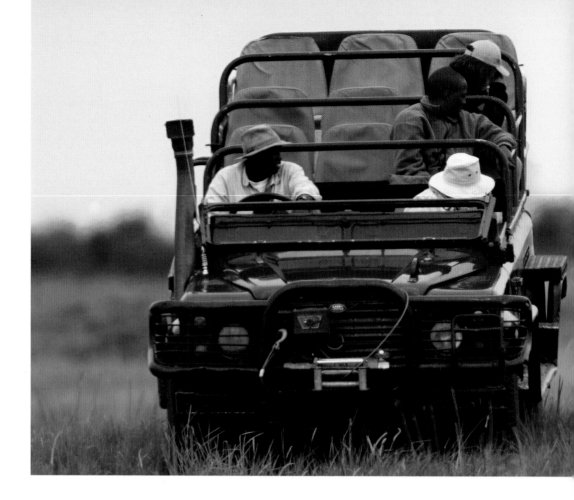

KEEP YOUR EYE ON THE LION

Want to visit your lion neighbors?

━━ **Track them down by looking for a trail of bent grass.**

━━ **Look for a pride resting under some shady trees. Don't make noise or talk when you find them. Lions don't like to be disturbed!**

am not really in charge." As a result, more fights break out and more disruption in the prides occurs.

When a lion is killed, naturally or by safari hunters, a new male comes in and takes over. Unfortunately, he immediately kills all the cubs. This allows the females to mate again, so the new male can raise his own cubs. As a result, each time a male lion is shot, up to 30 other lions might die.

We strongly believe that lions need to be in the wild. Today, however, many parks are just getting too small. So to save a lion, we have to save the land first. We may have to set aside more wildlife land. But that doesn't mean we have to kick all the people out of the way. Beverly and I live in the bush quite peacefully with lions around us every day. We may be an exception, of course, because we work with lions and have studied their behavior.

Some Africans raise cattle. Cattle and lions don't mix well, though. Cows are not native to Africa. They don't know how to defend themselves against

When the sun goes down, the heat subsides. Every-thing relaxes just a bit. Lions go on the prowl again, roused from their daylight sleep. They are ready to patrol their territory and disappear into the darkness. Our job is to make sure they don't disappear forever.

big predators. To the lion, cows are easy prey! But if the cattle are kept in a safe place at night and are watched in the day, lions and cattle can coexist.

Tourism is one thing that can help save the lions. Tourist lodges have been successful in Botswana. Travelers come to Africa on safari to see and photo-graph lions. They pay the lodge, and the local peo-ple get some money, too. The villagers build schools and clinics with these tourist dollars. They realize that lions can help them earn money.

Today there may be fewer than 25,000 wild lions left on Earth. There have never been as few as there are today. They are disappearing.

Lions can teach us how to behave in a gentler way toward the Earth. They don't run around slaughtering everything in their paths—even though they could. A little more compassion and friendliness will help save the world in the end.

25

HOW YOU CAN HELP

▼ *Having a younger brother can be a pain in the neck! Especially if he has teeth like knives, claws like needles, and way too much energy.*

▬ Our "ecological footprint" describes how much space on Earth each of us needs. It includes the land we need to grow food, the carbon we release, the water we use, and our living space. Each person needs two and a half acres. This means the Earth is already too small. See what you can do each day to reduce the impact that you have on the Earth. Recycle. Find out about global warming. Don't waste food or water. If we don't change, it won't just be the lions that run out of space!

▬ Think about how your actions affect the planet. If you throw a soda can out of the car window, who will pick it up? Will it land in the gutter and stay there, attracting rats and other creatures? Will it wash down into the sewer and make its way into a river or the sea? How long will it remain there?

▬ Saving lions starts at home. They need wild land. If we use up every piece of natural space, there will be more pressure on all wildlife.

▬ National Geographic's Conservation Trust is raising money to save lions in places like Kenya and Botswana. Maybe your parents would want to send them a donation, or maybe you could sometimes send them your allowance. Go to www.nationalgeographic.com /donate/conserveafrica.html.

▬ Read as much as you can about lions. This knowledge could prepare you for encounters if you do go to Africa one day. It could even help you when dealing with any cat or wild animal.

IT'S YOUR TURN

You can see many of these lion behaviors in a zoo. You can watch lions at rest or cubs playing, or hear a big male roar. Practice recognizing individual animals. Maybe one has a black-tipped tail, one has a notched ear, or one is very small. Once you know each of them, you will start to see how they act within the group. It takes a lot of patience. Don't make noises to disturb the lions. You want to see them behaving naturally. You may have to watch for a long time.

Now that you know a lot about lions, would you like to observe them yourself? You can see lions in many zoos. And maybe someday you can go to Africa to see and photograph wild lions.

What interests you most about lions? Cubs playing or learning to hunt? Females raising their young? The males displaying their handsome manes?

Take pictures and write captions about what each photo shows, including where and when you took it. A video camera can be fun to use too!

➡ *We called this female cub Princess. When she slipped and nearly fell from a tree, she actually looked embarrassed.*

FACTS
AT A
GLANCE

⬇ *These playful lion cubs will grow up to be fierce predators, weighing up to 420 pounds (about 191 kg).*

▬ Scientific Name
Panthera leo

▬ Common Names
We sometimes refer to lions as big cats. In Africa, the lion has a few other names. In Botswana, we call them Tau. In Kenya, it is Simba. But when I see a huge lion, I usually just say, "Wow!"

▬ Features
Of the classic tawny-skinned cats of Africa, females weigh in around 270–300 lbs (122–136 kg) and males weigh about 330–420 lbs (150–191 kg). In the swamps of Botswana's Okavango, they are about 15 percent larger because of their diet of buffalo. Females are less than 9 ft (2.75 m) long. Males are up to 10 ft (3 m) long. Another feature of lions is their tremendous roar. Both male and female lions have a powerful roar that can be heard up to 5 miles (8 km) away. It is not always one burst of sound. Sometimes it's a series: *ROAR, uf, uf, uf, uf.* If you're standing close by, it can actually hurt

your head as the sound waves vibrate in your skull.

▬ Diet
Lions eat just about anything, from mouse-like rodents called shrews to buffalo and elephants. But they prefer medium-sized prey like zebra and wildebeest. In Botswana, we have always found that they prefer buffalo.

▬ Reproduction
Mating takes place over a full week. They don't feed at all during this time. Females carry the young for about 108 days on average. Litters consist of about three or four cubs. Cubs are often born blind, or with milky, grey-blue eyes. They get black patches on the backs of their ears and tail tufts at five weeks. A five-week-old lion cub's paws are the size of those of a fully grown male leopard.

▬ Status in the Wild
There are about 25,000 lions today in the wild. This is fewer than at any time in the history

of lions. But lions are quite difficult to count accurately, so we may have more—or less! They range from the tip of Africa to the southern reaches of the Sahara and from the east to west coasts. There is even a small group of lions in the Gir Forest in India. This is a remnant population of a few hundred. They are all that's left from the days of old when lions spread right across Africa and Asia. The population in general has seriously declined.

Threats

"Canned" lion hunting and captive breeding have placed over 3,000 lions behind bars in Africa. The canned hunting industry allows trophy hunters without the time, bravery, sense of what's right, or even sportsmanship to buy a lion in a cage, often hand-reared, and to shoot it. They then pretend that they had been on safari in Africa. This practice is now largely being banned.

Lifespan

In captivity, lions lead pampered lives. Hunting is just a distant dream. They are much like domestic cats in this way. They can live into their 30s. But in the harsh wild world of Africa, where they have to hunt for food, lions live up to 15 years.

Home ranges

The lions we follow in Botswana have about 120 square miles (310 sq km) of range for each pride. Males sometimes dominate two or even three female groups. They have extended ranges, but it depends on the habitat. In thick forests or swamps, lions have smaller territories and home ranges. In open plains their range expands.

A lion shakes pesky flies away.

GLOSSARY

Carnivore: an animal that eats mainly other animals.

Clan: a group of animals like hyenas that are related. They live and hunt together throughout their lives.

Cub: a young lion, from birth to age 18 months.

Nomadic: of lions, wandering without a fixed territory.

Predator: an animal that preys on other animals as food.

Pride: a group of lions that live and hunt together.

Safari: means "journey" in Swahili; in English, refers to an expedition into wildlife areas of Africa to photograph, observe, or conduct a hunt for trophies.

Savanna: a tropical grassland with scattered trees.

Territory: the area that one pride of lions lives in, hunts in, and defends.

FIND OUT MORE

Books & Articles

Bertram, Brian. *Lions.* Stillwater, MN: Voyageur Press, 1998.

Elwood, Ann, & Estrada, Jackie. *Lions. Zoobooks,* Volume 6, Number 9, 1989.

Joubert, Dereck and Beverly. *African Diaries.* National Geographic Society, 2000.

Joubert, Dereck and Beverly. *Hunting with the Moon.* Washington, D.C.: National Geographic Society, 1997.

Joubert, Dereck and Beverly. *Relentless Enemies: Lions and Buffalo.* Washington, D.C.: National Geographic Society, 2006.

Kat, Pieter, & Harvey, Chris. *Prides: The Lions of Moremi.* Washington, D.C.: Smithsonian Institution Press, 2000.

Schaller, George. *Serengeti Lion.* Chicago: Chicago University Press, 1976.

Web Sites

http://nationalzoo.si.edu/Animals/GreatCats/lionfacts.cfm

www.lionresearch.org

Defenders of Wildlife:
http://www.defenders.org/

IUCN (International Union for the Conservation of Nature and Natural Resources):
http://www.iucn.org/

National Wildlife Federation:
http://www.nwf.org/

World Wildlife Fund:
http://www.worldwildlife.org/

◄ *Mr. Lion kicking back with a pal.*

INDEX

Illustrations are indicated by **boldface.**

RESEARCH & PHOTOGRAPHIC NOTES

So you want to photograph lions and big African wildlife? Imagine sitting in 128°F temperatures in the blazing sun for 12 hours straight, waiting for the kill. One time, the lions we'd been watching for days were all in position. We had so many cameras ready that the vehicle looked like a military gunship. Beverly's three Canon digital cameras with 600mm, 400mm, and wide-angle lenses were laid out on beanbags and tripods for stability. Each has a filter and lens hood to stop the sun flaring against the lens. I film with a big HD video camera and a massive lens on a tripod head mounted to the side of the vehicle. Suddenly the lions sprang, attacking the buffalo and isolating three bulls at the back of the herd. It was a fast-running chase. I was filming and Beverly was snapping away. The lioness came in like a bullet, gaining ground, getting closer and closer. She coiled up and launched herself into the air and then … nothing! The frame went black! My battery went dead at the exact instant of the attack! I grabbed a new battery, jammed it into place, and fired up the camera. I focused and started filming again … only to see that it was all over! Whenever this happens, Beverly and I give it some time and then laugh. If we didn't, we would hurl our cameras out of the car. Laughing at life and at ourselves seems to make it all okay. And it *is* okay—we'll be back again tomorrow!

THIS BOOK IS DEDICATED TO LIONS.

Dear Lion, We thank you for all the opportunities, all the laughter and fun you have brought to our lives, and all the happiness and understanding we have been able to pass on to the world. In the same way, we must apologize for all the things we do to you as Man. Mostly we are ignorant twits, but sometimes we get it right.

The National Geographic Society deserves special thanks for its support over 25 years of lion work. I also wish to thank the President of Botswana, Fests Mogae, the Vice President Lt. Gen. Ian Khama, the Department of Wildlife and National Parks, its director, and staff; and the people of Botswana, who have all adopted us as two weird lion people. I was named Radetau, "father of the lions" in Setswana, by the people of Botswana, but in so many ways we are Bana ba Botswana, "children of Botswana," and very grateful of that. Words struggle not to fall over themselves as poor and shabby half-cousins in the shadow of great images like the photography Beverly creates, and a book like this would be less colorful (although cheaper) without her pictures. Besides that, she is my soul mate, and a beautiful person inside and out.

Book design by David M. Seager The body text of the book is set in ITC Century. The display text is set in Knockout and Party Noid.

Published by the National Geographic Society

John M. Fahey, Jr., *President and Chief Executive Officer*

Gilbert M. Grosvenor, *Chairman of the Board*

Nina D. Hoffman, *Executive Vice President; President, Book Publishing Group*

Staff for This Book

Nancy Laties Feresten, *Vice President, Editor-in-Chief of Children's Books*

Bea Jackson, *Design and Illustrations Director, Children's Books*

Jennifer Emmett, Mary Beth Oelkers-Keegan, *Project Editors*

David M. Seager, *Art Director*

Lori Epstein, *Illustrations Editor*

Jocelyn G. Lindsay, *Researcher*

Jean Cantu, *Illustrations Specialist*

Carl Mehler, *Director of Maps*

Rebecca Baines, *Editorial Assistant*

R. Gary Colbert, *Production Director*

Lewis R. Bassford, *Production Manager*

Maryclare Tracy, Nicole Elliott, *Manufacturing Managers*

Cover: Face to face with the master of the savanna. *Back Cover:* Beverly and Dereck Joubert look comfortable posing for the camera, and so do the lions behind them. *Page One:* This playful cub will grow up to be a determined hunter. *Title Page:* A lion fixes his intelligent gaze on a distant object. *Credits Page:* A lioness bares her razor-sharp teeth.

Library of Congress Cataloging-in-Publication Data

Joubert, Beverly.
 Face to face with lions / by Beverly and Dereck Joubert.
   p. cm.
 ISBN 978-1-4263-0207-7 (trade) -- ISBN 978-1-4263-0208-4 (lib.)
 1. Lions--Africa. I. Joubert, Dereck. II. Title. III. Title: Lions.
QL737.C23J685 2008
599.757--dc22

2007011118

Founded in 1888, the National Geographic Society is one of the largest nonprofit scientific and educational organizations in the world. It reaches more than 285 million people worldwide each month through its official journal, NATIONAL GEOGRAPHIC, and its four other magazines; the National Geographic Channel; television documentaries; radio programs; films; books; videos and DVDs; maps; and interactive media. National Geographic has funded more than 8,000 scientific research projects and supports an education program combating geographic illiteracy.

For more information, please call 1-800-NGS LINE (647-5463) or write to the following address:

National Geographic Society
1145 17th Street N.W.
Washington, D.C. 20036-4688 U.S.A.

Visit us online at
www.nationalgeographic.com/books

For information about special discounts for bulk purchases, please contact National Geographic Books Special Sales: ngspecsales@ngs.org

Printed in China

The publisher gratefully acknowledges the assistance of Christine Kiel, K-3 Curriculum and Reading Consultant, and of Ilaria Di Silvestre, Park W/ECOPAS Programme, for expert consultation on the map.